Lerner **SPORTS**™

GREATEST OF ALL TIME PLAYERS

G.O.A.T. BASKETBALL SIXTH PLAYERS

Audrey Stewart

Lerner Publications ◆ Minneapolis

SPORTS THRILLS MEET RESEARCH SKILLS

Lerner SPORTS

Free Database Trial: **lernersports.com**

Lerner Publications Company
An imprint of Lerner Publishing Group, Inc.
241 First Avenue North
Minneapolis, MN 55401 USA

For reading levels and more information, look up this title at www.lernerbooks.com.

Main body text set in Aptifer Sans LT Pro.
Typeface provided by Linotype AG.

Library of Congress Cataloging-in-Publication Data

Names: Stewart, Audrey (Children's author), author.
Title: G.O.A.T. basketball sixth players / Audrey Stewart.
Other titles: Greatest of all time basketball sixth players
Description: Minneapolis, MN : Lerner Publications, [2025] | Series: Greatest Of All Time players | Includes bibliographical references and index. | Audience: Ages 7–11 | Audience: Grades 2–3 | Summary: "Sixth players start games on the bench, but they can still have a huge impact on basketball games. Read about the best sixth players in basketball history. Then make your own G.O.A.T. list!"—Provided by publisher.
Identifiers: LCCN 2023048817 (print) | LCCN 2023048818 (ebook) | ISBN 9798765625798 (library binding) | ISBN 9798765628751 (paperback) | ISBN 9798765633687 (epub)
Subjects: LCSH: Basketball players—Biography—Juvenile literature.
Classification: LCC GV884.A1 .S78 2025 (print) | LCC GV884.A1 (ebook) | DDC 796.323092/273—dc23/eng/20231130

LC record available at https://lccn.loc.gov/2023048817
LC ebook record available at https://lccn.loc.gov/2023048818

Manufactured in the United States of America
1 – CG – 7/15/24

TABLE OF CONTENTS

Los Angeles Clippers sixth player Lou Williams takes a shot during a 2017 game against the Washington Wizards.

THE MOST VALUABLE PLAYERS

The Washington Wizards were playing the Los Angeles Clippers on December 9, 2017. It was a close game. The Clippers were down 109–107 with 12 seconds on the game clock. A three-pointer gave the Clippers the lead. But the Wizards answered with a basket and a free throw to go ahead 112–110.

FACTS AT A GLANCE

» **ANDRE IGUODALA** IS ONE OF ONLY 10 PLAYERS TO PLAY IN SIX STRAIGHT NATIONAL BASKETBALL ASSOCIATION (NBA) FINALS.

» **J. R. SMITH** WAS A FIRST-ROUND NBA DRAFT PICK OUT OF HIGH SCHOOL IN 2004.

» **DEWONNA BONNER** WON THE WOMEN'S NATIONAL BASKETBALL ASSOCIATION (WNBA) SIXTH PLAYER OF THE YEAR AWARD IN 2009, 2010, AND 2011.

» **JAMAL CRAWFORD** HOLDS THE NBA RECORD FOR MOST POINTS IN A GAME BY A SIXTH PLAYER. HE SCORED 51 POINTS AGAINST THE DALLAS MAVERICKS IN 2019.

With 2.8 seconds left, Clippers sixth player Lou Williams shot the ball. He hit a three-pointer, and the Clippers won 113–112. Williams didn't just score the game-winning basket. He had 35 points and eight assists in the game. He scored more than 30 percent of his team's total points.

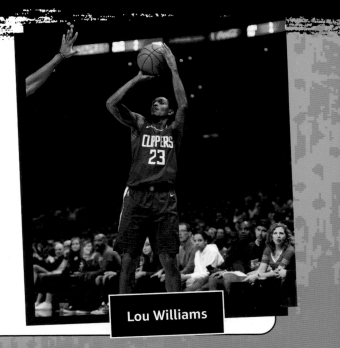

Lou Williams

Sixth players begin the game on the bench. They enter the game later to score, grab rebounds, and play tough defense. Sixth players are first to enter the game from the bench. They often come into games when one of the five starting players becomes tired.

Tyler Herro started in just 10 games for the Miami Heat in the 2021–2022 season, but he still averaged 20.7 points per game.

In his first two full seasons with the Utah Jazz, Jordan Clarkson only started two games. He was the NBA Sixth Man of the Year in 2020–2021.

But sixth players do a lot more than simply give the starters a break. The best sixth players can give their team a huge boost. They enter the game with energy after resting on the bench. Sixth players can score quickly or play tough defense against a tired opponent. Having a skilled sixth player shows a team's strength beyond their starting five. Sometimes the best sixth players play more than some of the starters.

LEANDRO BARBOSA

The Phoenix Suns got better right away when Leandro Barbosa joined the team in 2003. He still holds the Suns record for most points scored by a rookie in their first start with 27. Barbosa's hard work and speed earned him the NBA Sixth Man of the Year award for the 2006–2007 season. His fast feet led him to a career high of 41 points in a 2009 win against the Oklahoma City Thunder.

Barbosa played for several teams before joining the Golden State Warriors in 2014. He won his first NBA championship with Golden State in 2015. In Game 5 of the NBA Finals, Barbosa scored 13 points while only playing 17 minutes of game time. Several of the team's starters played more than 40 minutes.

Barbosa returned to the Suns in 2016–2017 to finish his NBA career. He scored a season-high 21 points in a game against the Los Angeles Lakers. He played his final game in March 2017. Barbosa ended his NBA career with 850 games played.

LEANDRO BARBOSA STATS

🏀	Points per Game	10.6
🏀	Rebounds per Game	2
🏀	Assists per Game	2.1
🏀	Field Goal Percentage	45.9

ANDRE IGUODALA

For 10 seasons in the NBA, Andre Iguodala was a successful starting player. But while playing for the Golden State Warriors in 2014–2015, new head coach Steve Kerr wanted Iguodala to try something new. Iguodala started most games on the bench during the next four seasons and averaged 3.8 rebounds and 7.1 points per game.

During the 2015 NBA Finals, Iguodala was one of Golden State's best players. He started three of the six games on the bench and still won the Finals Most Valuable Player (MVP) award. He averaged 16.3 points, four assists, and 5.8 rebounds during the 2015 Finals and helped the Warriors win their first title in 40 years. In 2015–2016, Iguodala finished second in Sixth Man of the Year voting. He helped the Warriors win the NBA title three more times before he retired in 2023. He is only the 10th player in history to play in six straight NBA Finals.

ANDRE IGUODALA STATS

🏀	Points per Game	11.3
🏀	Rebounds per Game	4.9
🏀	Assists per Game	4.2
🏀	Field Goal Percentage	46.3

Stats are accurate through the 2022–2023 NBA season.

MONTREZL HARRELL

After his second year at the University of Louisville, Montrezl Harrell was one of the top college players in the US. He was a member of the American Athletic Conference All-Conference First Team. Some fans thought he might enter the NBA Draft after two years at Louisville. But Harrell chose to stay in college and play another season.

The Houston Rockets drafted Harrell in 2015. After two seasons with Houston, he joined the Los Angeles Clippers. Harrell scored a career-high 34 points in a 2019 Clippers loss to the Milwaukee Bucks. He tied his own record in a 134–109 win against the New Orleans Pelicans.

During the 2018–2019 season, Harrell came into the game from the bench in all but five games for the Clippers. He averaged 16.6 points in 26.3 minutes per game. Harrell won the NBA Sixth Man of the Year award in 2020. He joined the Philadelphia 76ers in 2022.

MONTREZL HARRELL STATS

 Points per Game		12.1
Rebounds per Game		5
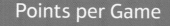 Assists per Game		1.3
Field Goal Percentage		61.9

Stats are accurate through the 2022–2023 NBA season.

KELSEY PLUM

In 2017, the San Antonio Stars picked Kelsey Plum first overall in the WNBA Draft. The Stars became the Las Vegas Aces the following year.

In Plum's second season with the Aces, the team finished second in their conference. They made the playoffs for the first time since 2014, but they lost to the Washington Mystics. Plum kept improving. In 2021, Plum started every game on the bench. She averaged 25.6 minutes of playing time per game. She had 14.8 points, 3.6 assists, and 2.5 rebounds per game. She also made 38.6 percent of her shots from the three-point line and 94.4 percent from the free throw line. Plum won the WNBA Sixth Player of the Year award that season.

Plum became a starter in 2022 and set career highs with 20.2 points per game. The Aces won the 2022 WNBA championship, and Plum played in her first WNBA All-Star Game. She won the All-Star MVP award after scoring 30 points. She helped the Aces win a second WNBA title in 2023.

KELSEY PLUM STATS

🏀	Points per Game	13.4
🏀	Rebounds per Game	2.5
🏀	Assists per Game	4
🏀	Field Goal Percentage	43.5

Stats are accurate through the 2023 WNBA season.

BRIONNA JONES

At the University of Maryland, Brionna Jones led all US college players by making 66.5 percent of her shots during the 2015–2016 season and 69 percent during the 2016–2017 season. She was a first-round pick in the 2017 WNBA Draft. She joined the Connecticut Sun.

The 2021–2022 season was her best year in the WNBA. She started all 32 games and averaged 14.7 points, 7.3 rebounds, and 1.8 assists. Jones played in her first WNBA All-Star Game in 2021. She also won the Most Improved Player award that season.

In 2022, Jones became her team's sixth player. She started just seven of the 36 games she played that season. She averaged 13.8 points, 5.1 rebounds, 1.3 assists, and 1.2 steals per game. Jones won the 2022 Sixth Player of the Year award and played in her second All-Star Game. That season, she ranked 17th in the WNBA for scoring, fifth in field goal percentage, and second for offensive rebounds. She did it all while averaging only 25.1 minutes of playing time per game.

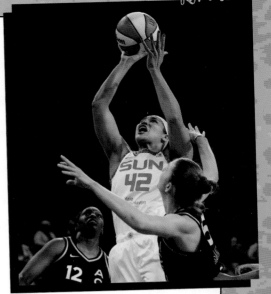

BRIONNA JONES STATS

🏀	Points per Game	9.2
🏀	Rebounds per Game	4.4
🏀	Assists per Game	1
🏀	Field Goal Percentage	56.3

Stats are accurate through the 2023 WNBA season.

J. R. SMITH

J. R. Smith joined the New Orleans Hornets right out of high school. He played two seasons with the Hornets before moving to the Denver Nuggets in 2006. During his time in Denver, Smith averaged 13.7 points per game and was a runner-up for the NBA Sixth Man of the Year award.

Smith became the first NBA player to record three career games with 10 or more three-pointers. In 2009, he played just over 29 minutes and had a career-high 45 points and 11 three-pointers in a Nuggets win over the Sacramento Kings.

Playing for the New York Knicks in 2012–2013, Smith averaged a career-high 18.1 points while starting all 80 games on the bench. He became the first sixth player in 23 years to have three 30-point games in a row. After winning NBA championships with the Cleveland Cavaliers and the Los Angeles Lakers, Smith announced his retirement from the league in 2020.

J. R. SMITH STATS

Points per Game	12.4
Rebounds per Game	3.1
Assists per Game	2.1
Field Goal Percentage	41.9

During college, DeWanna Bonner played two years for USA Basketball. She helped her team win the FIBA Under-21 World Championship in 2007. Her WNBA career began in 2009 with the Phoenix Mercury. As a sixth player, Bonner averaged 11.2 points and 21.3 minutes per game and won her first WNBA championship. She won the WNBA Sixth Player of the Year award in 2009, 2010, and 2011.

In 2014, Bonner won her second championship with Phoenix. She was part of the All-WNBA First Team in 2015 and has been a WNBA All-Star five times. Bonner played 10 seasons with the Mercury. She joined the Connecticut Sun in 2020. Bonner scored a career-high 41 points in a 2023 win over the Las Vegas Aces. Bonner is the first player in Sun history to have back-to-back 30-point games.

DEWANNA BONNER STATS

Points per Game	14.9
Rebounds per Game	6.1
Assists per Game	2.3
Field Goal Percentage	41.6

Stats are accurate through the 2023 WNBA season.

Malcolm Brogdon was Atlantic Coast Conference Player of the Year and Defensive Player of the Year during his 2015–2016 season with the University of Virginia Cavaliers. He is the first player to earn both awards in the same season. Brogdon was a second-round pick of the Milwaukee Bucks in the 2016 NBA Draft. In his first NBA season, Brogdon started 47 of his 75 games on the bench. He averaged 10.2 points, 2.8 rebounds, and 4.2 assists per game. Brogdon won the Rookie of the Year award that season and was part of the NBA All-Rookie First Team.

Brogdon joined the Boston Celtics in 2022. He averaged 14.9 points, 4.2 rebounds, and 3.7 assists per game in the 2022–2023 season. In a January 2023 game against the Charlotte Hornets, he started the game on the bench and scored a season-high 30 points. Brogdon won the NBA Sixth Man of the Year award in 2023.

MALCOLM BROGDON STATS

Points per Game	15.4
Rebounds per Game	4.2
Assists per Game	4.6
Field Goal Percentage	46.7

Stats are accurate through the 2022–2023 NBA season.

LOU WILLIAMS

At 6 feet 1 (1.9 m) and 175 pounds (79.4 kg), Lou Williams is smaller than most other NBA sixth players. He started his NBA career in 2005 with the Philadelphia 76ers. In 2011–2012, his final season with the 76ers, he was a Sixth Man of the Year award runner-up. Williams led the team in scoring with 14.9 points per game.

Between 2012 and 2017, Williams played for four different teams, including the Atlanta Hawks and the Toronto Raptors. He won his first Sixth Man of the Year award in 2015 while playing for the Raptors. Williams began every game on the bench and averaged 25.2 minutes of playing time per game. In a 2018 game against the Golden State Warriors, Williams scored a career-high 50 points in 35 minutes. Williams is tied with Jamal Crawford for the most NBA Sixth Man of the Year awards with three. Williams is the NBA's all-time leading scorer off the bench. He retired from playing in June 2023.

LOU WILLIAMS STATS

Points per Game		13.9
Rebounds per Game		2.2
Assists per Game		3.4
Field Goal Percentage		41.9

JAMAL CRAWFORD

Jamal Crawford played for nine different teams in 21 NBA seasons. For most of his career, he started many games on the bench. Crawford began his career with the Chicago Bulls in 2000. After four seasons, he joined the New York Knicks and averaged 17.6 points per game.

A big moment in Crawford's career was in 2014 when he played for the Los Angeles Clippers. It was a close game against the Toronto Raptors. Crawford scored season highs with 37 points and 11 assists in 32 minutes of playing time. He helped the Clippers beat the Raptors by eight points. And in 2019, Crawford set the NBA record for most points by a sixth player in a single game with 51. He started the game on the bench and played 38 total minutes against the Mavericks.

Crawford and Lou Williams are tied for most NBA Sixth Man of the Year awards with three. Crawford is the eighth player in NBA history to play for at least 20 seasons. He retired from playing in 2022.

JAMAL CRAWFORD STATS

Points per Game	14.6
Rebounds per Game	2.2
Assists per Game	3.4
Field Goal Percentage	41

EVEN MORE G.O.A.T.

There have been so many amazing sixth players in NBA and WNBA history. Choosing only 10 is a challenge. Here are 10 others who could have made the G.O.A.T. list.

No. 11	MANU GINOBILI
No. 12	KEVIN MCHALE
No. 13	BILL WALTON
No. 14	RICKY PIERCE
No. 15	JAMES HARDEN
No. 16	JASON TERRY
No. 17	DEARICA HAMBY
No. 18	ALLIE QUIGLEY
No. 19	RODNEY ROGERS
No. 20	ERIC GORDON

YOUR
G.O.A.T.

It's your turn to make a G.O.A.T. list about sixth players. Start by doing research. Consider the rankings in this book. Then check out the Learn More section on page 31. Explore the books and websites to learn more about basketball players of the past and present.

You can search online for more information about great players too. Check with a librarian, who may have other resources for you. You might even try reaching out to basketball teams or players to see what they think.

Once you're ready, make your list of the greatest players of all time. Then ask people you know to make G.O.A.T. lists and compare them. Do you have players no one else listed? Are you missing anybody your friends think is important? Talk it over and try to convince them that your list is the G.O.A.T.!

GLOSSARY

assist: a pass from a teammate that leads directly to a score

defense: the team trying to stop the other team from scoring

draft: when teams take turns choosing new players

field goal: a basket scored when the ball is in play

free throw: an open shot taken from behind a line on the court after a foul by an opponent

opponent: a player on the opposing team

rebound: grabbing and controlling the ball after a missed shot

rookie: a first-year player

three-pointer: a shot taken from behind a line on the court that counts for three points

LEARN MORE

Brionna Jones
https://www.wnba.com/player/1628280/brionna-jones

Kortemeier, Todd, and Josh Anderson. *Inside the NBA Finals*. Parker, CO: The Child's World, 2023.

NBA Awards—Sixth Man of the Year
https://www.espn.com/nba/history/awards/_/id/40

O'Neal, Ciara. *The WNBA Finals*. Mendota Heights, MN: Apex, 2023.

Scheff, Matt. *NBA and WNBA Finals: Basketball's Biggest Playoffs*. Minneapolis: Lerner Publications, 2021.

Women's National Basketball Association Facts for Kids
https://kids.kiddle.co/Women%27s_National_Basketball_Association

INDEX

PHOTO ACKNOWLEDGMENTS

Image credits: Icon Sportswire/Contributor/Getty Images, p.4; Icon Sportswire/Contributor/Getty Images, p.5; Michael Reaves/Stringer/Getty Images, p.6; Chris Gardner/Stringer/Getty Images, p.7; Thearon W. Henderson/Contributor/Getty Images, p.8; Ezra Shaw/Staff/Getty Images, p.9; Ezra Shaw/Staff/Getty Images, p.10; Justin Ford/Contributor/Getty Images, p.11; Mitchell Leff/Contributor/Getty Images, p.12; Nic Antaya/Contributor/Getty Images, p.13; Ethan Miller/Staff/Getty Images, p.14; Michelle Farsi/Contributor/Getty Images, p.15; Mitchell Layton/Contributor/Getty Images, p.16; Ethan Miller/Staff/Getty Images, p.17; Doug Pensinger/Staff/Getty Images, p.18; Jason Miller/Contributor/Getty Images, p.19; Alex Slitz/Contributor/Getty Images, p.20; Ethan Miller/Staff/Getty Images, p.21; Megan Briggs/Stringer/Getty Images, p.22; Kevin C. Cox/Staff/Getty Images, 23; Vaughn Ridley/Contributor/Getty Images, p.24; Rocky Widner/Contributor/Getty Images, p.25; Manuela Davies/Contributor/Getty Images, p.26; Harry How/Staff/Getty Images, p.27

Cover: Jayne Kamin-Oncea/Contributor/Getty Images; Gregory Shamus/Staff Getty Images; Ethan Miller/Staff Getty Images